MINDFULNESS MEDITATION FOR SELF-HEALING

Beginner's Meditation Guide to Eliminate Stress and Anxiety, and Find Inner Peace and Happiness

Sarah Rowland

Copyright © **2017** **by** Sarah Rowland

All rights reserved. No part of this book may be reproduced or transmitted in any form or by any means, electronic or mechanical, including photocopying, recording or by any information storage and retrieval system without written permission of the publisher, except for the inclusion of brief quotations in a review.

TABLE OF CONTENTS

INTRODUCTION 1

Chapter 1 *Understanding Mindfulness Meditation* 3

Chapter 2 *Mindfulness Meditation Basics* 9

Chapter 3 *Mindfulness During Your Commute* 20

Chapter 4 *Mindfulness On The Bus Or Train* 33

Chapter 5 *Mindfulness At Work* 39

Chapter 6 *Mindfulness At Home* 48

Chapter 8 *Tips For Improving Your Ability To Be Mindful* 66

Conclusion 74

INTRODUCTION

Congratulations on downloading *Mindfulness Meditation for Self-Healing: Beginner's Meditation Guide to Eliminate Stress and Anxiety, and Find Inner Peace and Happiness*, and thank you for doing so. By picking up this book you are already well on your way to living in the moment more fully than you have ever thought possible and in so doing improve the quality of your life in a wide variety of different ways, some of which are sure to surprise you.

In order to help you along on your path to enlightenment, the following chapters will discuss everything you need to know to get started practicing mindfulness meditation, not just in a quiet place that is free from distractions, but at virtually any point throughout the day, no matter how hectic or stressful the situation might seem at first glance. First you will learn all about the history of mindfulness meditation as it has been practiced throughout the ages before next learning about the basics of the practice and how you can use it to become connected to the present in a deep and meaningful way.

From there you will then learn how to take advantage of the benefits that mindfulness meditation provides during your daily commute, while you are utilizing public transportation, while you are at work and while you are at home going about your daily routine. Finally, you will learn several tips and tricks that are sure to make the process of getting mindful as quick and painless as possible.

There are plenty of books on this subject on the market, thanks again for choosing this one! Every effort was made to ensure it is full of as much useful information as possible, please enjoy!

CHAPTER 1
Understanding Mindfulness Meditation

While it has been a part of the Buddhist faith for more than two thousand years, mindfulness meditation has become exceedingly popular in the Western world over the past several decades thanks to its proven ability to improve mental health including the treatment of stress, anxiety and even drug addiction. Professor Jon Kabat-Zinn brought the process to the attention of the modern world in the 1970s by publishing findings that linked it to stress reduction. This, in turn, lead to a flurry of new interest in the practice and a new understanding of the myriad of different ways that being mindful can help improve one's health by directly combating numerous different ailments. Studies on the topic have even proven so conclusive that it is now common to see mindfulness meditation being practiced everywhere from hospitals to prisons to veteran associations.

Since its inception, mindfulness meditation been proven via scientific study to improve the physical wellbeing of those that practice it on a regular basis. At its heart, mindfulness meditation is all about focusing your mind to ensure that you are as fully aware of each moment as fully as possible. This, in turn, allows you to exist more completely in any given moment by expanding your consciousness to the fullest.

While it might sound like a tall order at first, the truth of the matter is that being mindful is a skill which means it can be improved by regular practice in much the same way as any other skill. Luckily, practicing mindfulness meditation is as easy as finding a few moments to focus solely on the present and the information that your senses are providing you in the moment. In fact, if you can find just fifteen minutes a day to practice, you will soon find that your overall stress is likely to decrease and your sense of self is likely to be at an all-time high. This isn't just an ephemeral feeling either, neuroimaging performed on those who practice mindfulness meditation on a regular basis shows that their minds actually process information more effectively, they are able to more easily regulate their emotions and their attention spans than those who do not make the practice a part of their daily routine.

Furthermore, the sooner you begin practicing mindfulness meditation, the greater the chance that doing so will ensure your brain retains more volume as you age, dramatically improving overall brain health as a result. This increased vitality also reaches the hippocampus which, in turn, makes it easier to learn and retain new information with minimal effort. At the same time, the amygdala becomes less active which means that the amount of fear, stress and anxiety that you experience will be decreased as well. Additionally, a daily dose of mindfulness meditation is enough to reduce the amount of cortisol, a hormone that increases stress levels, that the body naturally produces.

In addition to the physical changes that you are likely to experience when meditating regularly, regularly practicing mindfulness meditation will also help you to more easily free your mind from any negative thought patterns you might otherwise find yourself getting stuck on making it easier to focus on the positive instead. Mindfulness meditation is so effective at this task that a recent study out of Johns Hopkins University actually found that it is just as effective at treating anxiety, depression and attention deficit disorder as many of the leading medications specifically designed to do the same thing. Another recent study also showed students preparing to take the Graduate Records Examination, the most common test to obtain admission into graduate school, who practiced mindfulness meditation regularly prior to testing scored approximately 10 percent better than their less mindful peers.

With so many physical and mental benefits, is it any wonder that mindfulness meditation is revered by Buddhists all around the world? The practice has its roots in a type of structured meditation called vipassana which, when translated, refers to a mental state that promotes living in the moment while still being aware of how the present and the future intertwine. Those who master vipassana are said to more fully understand the universe as a whole as well as their place in it.

In order to reach a state of vipassana, practitioners strive for what are known as the three marks of existence: impermanence, non-self and dissatisfaction, which together are believed to bring unity to all living things. Non-self refers to the idea of understanding the boundaries between the self and the physical world with the understanding that coming to terms with these boundaries make it easier to fully grasp the intricacies of both. Meanwhile, dissatisfaction refers to the innate desire seek satisfaction from fleeting experiences and the inevitable feeling that losing these things creates. This leads into the idea of importance as only by accepting the temporary nature of life can true happiness and inner peace be found.

Other reasons to practice mindfulness meditation

- Mindfulness meditation naturally leads to a deeper understanding of the self and allows many people to take stock of their strengths and weaknesses, leading to personal growth.

- Studies show that those who practice mindfulness regularly have a stronger memory, leading to an easier retention of facts in both the long and the short term.

- In addition to the specifics, mindfulness meditation improves overall physical wellbeing with those who practice regularly reporting fewer instances of illness and a more rapid recovery when they do fall ill.

- Mindfulness meditation can help improve emotional control while at the same time increasing one's threshold for pain.

- As surprising as it might seem, making a habit of being mindful can actually make even the most middling music seem more engaging. This deeper level of engagement leads to a general increase of enjoyment, regardless of the type of music or any previous musical preferences.

- With a regular dose of mindfulness meditation, many people experience a dramatic increase in their ability to empathize with others no matter what the situation. Furthermore, it allows practitioners to listen to other viewpoints more actively, more compassionately and results in their ability to withhold judgement on thoughts and ideas that differ from their own.

CHAPTER 2
Mindfulness Meditation Basics

While looking inside yourself with the idea of finding an untapped well of inner peace and tranquility might seem daunting at first, rest assured that it is something anyone can achieve if they dedicate time and mental energy to practice mindfulness meditation every day. What's more, after you get the basics down you will find that almost any situation easily lends itself to being mindful if you simply commit yourself to being fully present in the moment and open yourself completely to the signals that your body is sending you.

While one of the best things about mindfulness meditation is its malleable nature, when you are first getting started it is recommended that you set some time aside each day to specifically devote to the practice. Ideally, this should be someplace that is quiet and during a period of time when you feel relaxed and where you can devote as much as thirty minutes to going deep within yourself without fear of worldly distractions. Remember, being mindful is all about creating space between the sensory information that your body is always sending to your mind and your reactions to that information so the less stimuli you have to deal with at the start, the easier you will find the practice to be.

Getting started

1. *Choose a set time and stick to it:* As with any burgeoning habit, it is important that you create a routine for your mindfulness meditation and stay with it if you hope for the practice to stick. It typically takes 30 days for a new habit to take root in your daily schedule which is why it is important to commit fully to practicing mindfulness meditation if you ever want it to become part of your routine. Due to its low impact nature, nothing external is required, it is very easy for many people to make excuses to get out of meditating, especially if their daily schedule is already filled to bursting.

If you find yourself always coming up with an excuse to get out of meditating in the moment, you may find the following piece of advice particularly useful. "Practice mindfulness meditation for fifteen minutes every day unless, of course, you are extremely busy in which case you should practice for thirty minutes instead." Don't let the outside world intrude on your potential for inner peace, find a time each day that works for you and stick with it no matter what; in a month's time, you will be glad you did.

2. *Get started by focusing on the moment:* While the ultimate goal of mindfulness meditation is to quiet the mind in an effort to find a state of internal calm despite the hustle and bustle of the outside world, many people find it difficult to achieve this state right out of the gate. Instead, you will likely find it easier to start to supplant any thoughts you might have by focusing all of your attention on the signals that your senses are relaying to you to the exclusion of everything else.

While you might not feel as though you are receiving much data on the physical world, especially if you are practicing in a quiet, temperate space, the truth of the matter is that your brain naturally filters out approximately eighty percent of everything it receives, you just need to get in the habit of tapping into it.

With practice, you will learn to tune out your more common thoughts and to instead tune into what is going on around you. When you do this, it is important to simply take in the information your senses are providing without thinking about it too deeply or passing judgement on what you perceive. Judging tends to lead to additional thoughts or, even worse, comparison of the present group of situations to those of the past which is more likely to pull you out of the moment and make finding the state of calm you are looking for even more difficult than it is likely to be, especially when you are just getting started.

Remember, the goal with mindfulness meditation is to get as close to existing in the moment as possible and ignoring everything outside of your current surroundings as much as possible. To reach the required state you are going to want to start by focusing on your breathing, the feel of the air slowly entering and exiting your lungs as well as any smells or tastes that go along with this practice. From there you can then expand the sphere of observation to any other sensations that your body might be experiencing, all the while going deeper into yourself in search of the point where your mind ceases to form new thoughts and simply exists in a state of peaceful relaxation.

3. *Make an effort to avoid judging what you feel:* When you first begin practicing mindfulness meditation it is perfectly natural for your mind to intrude with thoughts about your current surroundings or to fill the void you are trying to achieve with a constant stream of consciousness. This occurs because over the years you

have trained your brain to constantly be moving from one thought to the next in a rush to reach some conclusion or another.

When you find these errant thoughts breaching your sense of mental calm it is important to not interact with them as much as possible and instead to let them simply float away without interacting with them. If you find yourself getting sidetracked it is important to not attach a judgment to what has happened and to instead simply center yourself once more and continue as before. While this step is the most difficult for many people, it is important to keep it up until it becomes second nature as any interaction with the stray thoughts, even if it is just to chastise yourself for getting off track is an easy way to let even more thoughts through which will make it more difficult to find the state of mind that you are looking for.

4. *Keep at it:* When you first begin practicing mindfulness meditation it is important to do so with the right level of expectations regarding your results. Specifically, you will want to keep in mind that your

mind is likely to wander frequently and that you will need to persevere through these periods if you are ever going to reach the level of mental quiet that you are looking for. To understand the ultimate mindset that you are striving for, you may find it helpful to consider the period of blankness the mind enters after a question has been asked but before the answer comes to you. Finding a way to reach this type of state is key to your long-term success.

When it comes to clearing the mind, some people find it helpful to visualize their thoughts as a stream of bubbles that they are watching flow past them; others visualize a gate coming down to block out the stream of consciousness entirely leaving the thoughts to pile up on the far side. While these visualizations can make it easier to be aware of stray thoughts without interacting with them it is important to not become too reliant on them as they are still thoughts and you ultimately want to do away with them once your mind has gotten used to the idea that it doesn't need to constantly be moving from one thought or another. However you manage it, it is important to not to worry about chastising yourself when stray thoughts do emerge and to instead simply acknowledge the lapse and then get back to what you were doing.

What to expect

While many of the benefits of mindfulness meditation include physical changes to the body, it can be difficult to track them without scientific or medical help. Instead, the first positive changes that you are going to likely notice are going to include changes to the mental conditioning you have been subjected too for your entire life. Living in a modern society typically leads to a desire to hide our flaws from others as well as ourselves and to treat uncomfortable thoughts and feelings in much the same way. This, in turn, leads to a desire to revise the truth and rewrite personal histories until they show things in a more flattering light. While not necessarily the most healthy way to handle issues, this common cultural habit is actually an offshoot of the instinctual primal desire towards flight or fight that help ancient humans avoid threats whether they were real or imaginary.

While it was this impulse that helped our ancient ancestors survive and thrive amongst harsh natural conditions, these days it is easy for it to instead lead to an undermining of the very traits and qualities that make us unique. This is perhaps mindfulness meditation's greatest benefit, it allows people to gain a deeper understanding of themselves which is the first step to a greater acceptance of both strengths and weakness and finding the best way to reconcile the two.

In place of this negative and potentially harmful mindset, regularly practicing mindfulness meditation can lead you to what is known as radical acceptance. Essentially it allows you to be more in touch with what you are experience and feeling in the moment without any of the negative filters imposed by society. Radical acceptance allows you to understand that just because you have the occasional negative thought or feeling doesn't mean that there is anything wrong with you and it is an amazing, and free experience. A major part of radical acceptance is embracing all of your firsthand experiences as they really are, something that learning to exist in the moment will make much easier than it otherwise might be. Additionally, you will find that you will soon have a greater tolerance for negative experiences, until you are ultimately able to let them occur without letting them impact your overall mental state.

This improved mental state comes as a natural side effect of learning to be nonjudgmental not just of your thoughts but your experience as well. Cultivating mindfulness means leaning heavily on the suspension of inner judgement which is a result of putting greater thought into your feelings, thoughts and reactions and why they make you feel the way they do.

Additionally, you will likely find that regularly practicing mindfulness meditation naturally improves your ability to be aware of your surroundings at all times, even when you feel otherwise occupied by specific thoughts or problems that you may be facing. Typically, most people are so focused on the mistakes they have made in the past or their plans for the future that they don't have any mental energy left over for the present. This is a precarious situation as it then becomes easy to miss out on all the pleasures of the present without even realizing what it is you are giving up in order to focus on the past which you cannot change or the future which is largely uncertain. Instead of existing in this mental fugue state, existing more frequently in the present allows you to strengthen your awareness of what is happening at any given moment, letting you take charge of your future in a more active way and banishing the specter of missed opportunities that so frequently hangs over the past.

This practice is what is known as meta-awareness which is a state where you are able to interact with your thoughts and feelings in a more objective and detached way. This, in turn, allows you to more accurately measure your experiences to determine how they are affecting your sense of self without the baggage that such things typically carry around with them. Essentially, meta-awareness allows you to view yourself in a detached and objective manner which can benefit virtually every aspect of your life.

CHAPTER 3
Mindfulness During Your Commute

If you are like most people then it is likely that you spend an hour, if not more, of your day commuting to and from work. Most people fill this time by listening to podcasts, cursing at their fellow commuters, catching a quick bite to eat, or, if they are less safety conscious, reading or shaving. While all of these things certainly help pass the time, they do little for their peace of mind or overall wellbeing. That's where practicing mindfulness meditation during the commute comes in as the repetitive nature of the drive is a perfect time to clear your mind and focus on achieving a state of mindfulness that will put other drivers to shame.

By practicing mindfulness meditation on the road, you will find that you arrive at work ready to meet the challenges of the day head on, and arrive home at the end of the day with a clear head and heart, with the cares of the day left somewhere on the turnpike. Practicing mindfulness meditation on the go will allow you to reach your destination in a calm and focused state, that allows the stresses of rush hour traffic to fade into the background. What's more, practicing mindfulness meditation will also ensure you drive as safely as possible because you will be completely focused on the moment and the traffic that surrounds you.

Morning Commute

In order to make the most of your commute you are going to want to practice mindfulness from the very first moment that you enter your vehicle. As such, the first thing that you will want to do is to announce your intention aloud to the universe to help you get into the right mindset from the start. With your intentions made plain, the next thing that you are going to want to do (even before starting your vehicle) is to take several deep breaths. This will allow you to focus your attention on the sensations that your senses are providing you in order to ensure that you are in the right mindset even before you hit the road.

During this period, you want to take special care to focus on your body and the way it feels as you sit in your seat, the way your hands feel on the steering wheel and the way the world around you looks as you stare out at it from behind the windshield. From there, let the sensations of feeling expand outward and downward so that you feel your feet and the pressure you exert on the pedals before starting your vehicle.

As you begin your commute you are going to want to pay special attention to everything that is going on around you, both to the vehicles that you are directly interacting with as well as the people on the sidewalk and the buildings and signs that you previously passed without giving them a second thought. While this is going on be sure to also give some attention to your eyes as they are taking everything in and your ears as they convey the sounds of hundreds, if not thousands, of other people all moving together in relative harmony. Focus on these things, and only these things while you drive and you will be surprised at how much less of a hassle waiting in traffic suddenly becomes.

While this might initially strike you as too simple in order to produce the type of results you are looking for, it is important to put your doubts aside and give it a try before writing it off completely. Remember, when you first get started, even if you have already begun practicing mindfulness meditation in other facets of your life, it is perfectly natural for a stream of thoughts to be running through your head. This is especially true when heading into work as there are likely more things that you need to do than there are hours in the day to do them. Nevertheless, it is important to put everything else aside and strive to remain in the moment as thoroughly as possible.

For most people, the work day is a time for constant multitasking and this typically begins before the day itself does in the form of one form of electronic communication or another. As such, if you find that you are having a hard time focusing on the task at hand during your commute it may help to make a conscious effort to limit your electronic communication to a set period of time in the morning and ignore it for the rest of your morning until you have reached your destination and are ready to shift your day into high gear. While it may be difficult to ignore all of your notifications at first, after a few weeks you will wonder how you ever functioned when you were so closely tethered to your smartphone.

Suggestions to improve your morning commute

- If you find it hard to get into the right mindset when the time comes to set off for work, consider working a few moments of mindfulness into your day as soon as you wake up. Use the first few moments of the day to stretch your senses, as it were, and try and take in as much information about your surroundings as possible.

Additionally, you may find it useful to take stock of the thoughts that are already running through your mind at this hour and consider how they may affect your morning both for good and for ill. Getting into the habit of running a pre-assessment will allow you to jump into the more productive aspects of mindfulness meditation as soon as you get in your vehicle.

- When you find yourself thinking negative thoughts about the upcoming work day you may find it helpful to avoid banishing them as soon as they appear.

Instead, you may want to try cognitively reframing whatever it is that you are thinking of in an effort to turn them around until you can view them in a more positive light. Not only will this help to make each day a little brighter, it will help you approach the day more confidentially and with prevent extra stress or anxiety from clouding your day before it even properly begins.

- Use every moment of gridlock and every red light as a moment to quickly close your eyes, take a deep breath and to refocus on the task at hand. The frequent stop-and-go creates a natural barrier for thoughts that may have slipped through your mental blockade and will help to ensure that you stay on task no matter what else may have grabbed your attention. Remember, your goal during this time is to focus on what your senses are telling you to the exclusion of all else.

- In order to ensure that your morning commute mindfulness session proceeds as smoothly as possible you are going to want to avoid thinking about work as much as possible, especially if something is going on that seems to naturally draw your attention. The pressures of the day can begin naturally building without you even realizing it, leaving you feeling beaten and worn down before the day even starts. Only by remaining vigilant can you stay focused on the moment in order to ensure that your day is ultimately as productive as possible. Taking the time to worry about problems that you can't solve until you get to work will gain you nothing and only make it more difficult for you to focus on the moment.

Evening Commute

While the goal of the morning mindfulness meditation commute is to focus your energy for the coming day, the goal of the afternoon mindfulness meditation commute is to provide you with an opportunity to relax and detox from the stress of the day to ensure that when you make it home your heart is light and your head is clear. When done properly it will ensure that the stress of the day has melted away entirely and that you are ready for whatever it is that the evening may throw at you. With enough practice, instead of dreading the evening commute and the barrier it represents between you and your free time, your evening commute will become a buffer between your happiness and the stresses of the outside world. Remember, practice makes perfect!

Once you reach your vehicle, the first thing that you are going to want to do is to take an extra moment or two to think about the day that is coming to an end and any particular sticking points that may have unpleasant ramifications for the future. Consider why these incidents are sticking in out in your mind and what emotions they have attached themselves to and how you may be able to turn things around tomorrow. With your mental inventory complete, you will them want to make a conscious effort to let all of the negative emotions that you are holding on to float away on the mental breeze. While clearing your head you are also going to want to make a conscious effort to relax, starting with your neck and working your way down your entire body.

Next you are going to want to slowly take several deep breaths. As you do so you are going to want to focus on the feeling of the air as it enters your lungs, filling them until they are full to bursting. As you exhale you are going to want to visualize any stress you may have picked up throughout the day leaving your body as you do so. Visualize the air circulating through your body and consider how the motion makes you feel, use this practice as a gateway to considering the rest of your body and get back in touch with the sensations that the workday may have otherwise dulled. Focus on each of your senses in turn and let them bring you more fully into the moment piece by piece.

Once you have returned to a state of mindfulness, feel the pressure of the seat on your person, the feel of your hands on the steering wheel and the pressure exerted by your foot (or feet) on the pedals. As you drive you are going to want to remain in the moment as completely as possible, blocking out any thoughts that may still linger relating to the workday that you have not yet managed to shake.

However, when you find yourself stopped in traffic or waiting for a red light, instead of refocusing on the task at hand you are going to want to instead focus on the tension that the day has left in your body and focus exclusively on letting go of it and helping your body to relax. Each time you come to a stop you will want to focus on a different part of your body that you can feel holding onto the day's tension and visualize it leaving the body as you begin moving again. Once again you will want to start with your neck and work through your body all the way to the tips of your toes. If you make it through your entire body before you make it home then start again and repeat the process. When you finally reach your destination take an extra moment to consider how much better you feel now than you did before you left work and make one last effort to leave any workday complaints at the office where they belong.

Suggestions to improve your evening commute

- While it is all well and good to try focus on leaving your negative thoughts at the office, it can frequently more difficult in practice than it is in theory. As such, if you find yourself clinging to a particularly negative thought despite your best efforts it is important to push it to the back of your mind instead of letting it drag down your entire commute and prevent you from reaching the state of mindfulness that you are aiming for. Failing to do so will only lead to an excess of tension that you will be unable to get rid of as your body follows your mind's lead. If you simply focus on your breathing and work at remaining in the moment as much as possible, nine times out of ten the thought will pass on its own.

- If you find that you are still unable to get the negative thought or thoughts to subside and allow you to go on your way unmolested, you may find it useful to instead bring the full of your focus to bear on it in an effort to find out just why this thought continues to stick in your mind. In most cases you will find that the thought has actually gathered a greater amount of importance in your mind and that the reality of the situation isn't nearly as bad as your stress, nerves and anxiety have made it out to be.

With a little extra thought, you can often formulate a plan of attack against the negative thought to ensure that when the situation where you actually have to deal with it finally arises you are more than to handle it in the best and most efficient way possible.

- If you are still having trouble letting the day go and regaining the state of mindfulness that you can more easily reach during your morning commute then you might find a mantra to be a good way to get your mind back on the right track. The following are common mindfulness mantras that can be useful in practically any situations:

May I understand my discomfort

May I discard my discomfort

May I be stress free, happy and anxiety free

The cares of the day are behind me

I am in charge of my own happiness

- It is important to keep in mind that there is more than one way to practice mindfulness meditation and that what works for someone else might not work for you. Regardless of what you need to do in order to get into the proper mindset, if it helps you reach a state of mindfulness then it can be considered mindfulness meditation. The only time you need to worry about doing something wrong is if you use the fact that it can sometimes be difficult to find a state of mindfulness as an excuse to give up on the practice completely.

Remember, practicing mindfulness is a long journey and it can take several months in order to truly understand yourself, don't get discouraged and keep up the good work.

CHAPTER 4
Mindfulness On The Bus Or Train

If you utilize public transportation you can take the time spent getting where you are going to practice mindfulness meditation as effectively as if you were sequestered peacefully in your own home. There is one caveat however, in order to practice mindfulness meditation effectively it is important that you feel comfortable in the space in which you find yourself. If you find yourself in a situation where something requires your full attention you will likely be unable to reach your full mindfulness meditation potential.

While listening to music while practicing mindfulness meditation in public is not recommended, you may find it helpful to wear headphones as this is a clear signal to those around you that you do not wish to be disturbed. Furthermore, you may find it helpful to set some type of timer as when you get into the zone while being mindful it can be easy to lose track of time.

With the preliminaries out of the way, the first thing that you are going to want to do is to plant your feet firmly a comfortable distance apart from one another whether you are standing or sitting. If standing, take care that you are in a place where you can easily keep your balance. With your feet firmly planted slowly stretch out your body so that you assume the proper posture for your current surroundings. Take a moment to feel your body move with the rhythm of the train/bus and consider how you are connected not just to the transportation you are riding but to all of those who are sharing the journey with you.

Once you feel that you are centered, choose a spot in front of you that is approximately three feet from your current position. Choose a spot that is close to the ground, perhaps just a foot or two above the floor of the bus or train. Slowly lower your eyes to this point on the ground without lowering your neck, it is important to maintain proper posture throughout the exercise. As you feel your eyes begin to dip towards the floor focus exclusively on all of the sensory information they are providing you. From there, slowly incorporate the sensations that are being provided by the rest of your senses.

In order to tune out all of the noise and movement that naturally comes with riding public transportation, focus on your breathing and concentrate on taking rhythmic deep breaths at a nice slow pace. Once you have found a rhythm that works for you consider one of the options below as a means of focusing your attention and attaining a state of mindfulness that might not seem possible otherwise. Remember, practicing mindfulness meditation while using public transportation is even trickier to get the hang of than the other types of mindfulness meditation discussed in these pages. Don't get discouraged if you can't clear your mind as easily as you may be able to elsewhere, as with any other skill practice makes perfect.

Ways to focus your attention

1. Depending on the quality of your ride, you may find that the sensation of movement that you are experiencing to be enough to allow you to focus on the moment. Your body will be constantly moving in this situation, providing you with plenty of sensations to

focus on. If you have to move around during your trip consider focusing on the similarities and differences that the two positions provide you. As you breathe deeply feel the movement coursing beneath your feet, up through your body and all the way to your arms. Use each stop as an opportunity to refocus yourself on the moment. Don't forget to pay enough attention to your other senses that you lose track of your stop!

2. Depending on the quality of your public transportation, you may find that smell is another great anchor to plant you firmly in the present. This is also great practice for taking in sensations without judging them as you are likely to smell plenty of things that are good as well as bad while utilizing public transportation. Rather than making judgement calls regarding particular smells, simply focus on each unique smell as it appears, without breaking out of the rhythm of your breathing.

3. If the public transportation that you are on is particularly raucous, or if you don't have any other way to keep track of how close you are to your stop, you can count the number of stops you have remaining and repeat the number over and over again in your mind until it forms a type of mantra. This method of keeping in touch with the moment can also be combined with one of the others for maximum effectiveness.

While on one hand, practicing mindfulness meditation while surrounded by so many people can present its own unique challenges, on the other hand it also provides you with a breadth of different sensory information that you are unlikely to get when practicing any other type of mindfulness meditation, including practicing during your commute. Instead of trying to tune everything around you out completely, a more effective choice is to embrace the chaos that surrounds you and use it as a way to drown out any particularly nagging thoughts that have been plaguing you.

Consider the other passengers for example, are they talking to other passengers, ask yourself what they look like, how they act, sound, smell etc. Each stop provides a host of new ways to focus your attention and thus remain in the moment easier. What's more you have more sensations to focus on as well. Focus on the temperature changes as you move along your route as that and any other sensations are likely to change at a moment's notice.

CHAPTER 5
Mindfulness At Work

If asked what the most stressful part of their day is, a vast majority of the population would answer the workday without hesitation and with good reason. The combination of increased responsibility coupled with a lack of control combines to form a perfect storm that naturally leads to high levels of stress, anxiety and tension, often without any relief in sight. Luckily, mindfulness meditation, when practiced discreetly, can not only help mitigate these symptoms, it can also make it easier to focus on a particularly arduous task or project, often leading to unexpected insight and outside of the box thinking. As an added bonus, the state of calm that practicing mindfulness provides, not to mention the boost it will provide to your ability to empathize with others, will surely help to make you extremely popular around the office.

While not possible with all professions, with practice you will find that you can squeeze in a few minutes of mindfulness meditation here and there throughout the day. While the individual efficacy of any particular mindfulness meditation session might be relatively minimal, the overall gestalt will lead to a sense of wellbeing that is greater than the sum of its overall parts. While it might seem difficult to deal with the demands of the day, the demands of your coworkers and everything else that life throws at you, you can consider each micro mindfulness meditation session as islands of calm in an otherwise choppy sea. Mindfulness in the workplace should be thought of as a tool that allows you to squeeze every bit of efficiency out of the workday as long as you think carefully about how to use it as effectively as possible.

If you have already used the period of time prior to arriving at work as an opportunity to practice mindfulness meditation then when you arrive at work you will ideally already be in a state that is primed for making the most of every moment. You can then keep the mindfulness mindset rolling by taking a minute or two between tasks to focus on your breathing and the sensory information that your body is providing you. This doesn't need to be an elaborate process, it can be as quick and as simple as it needs to be. Remember, in this instance quantity definitely trumps quality. Make a point of practicing every day, but if you miss a day, don't use it as an excuse to form unproductive habits, simply pick up where you left off and start again.

Many people find that clearing their minds at work can be exceedingly difficult. If your job leaves you precious little time to sneak in a little mindfulness meditation then your best bet is going to be to start slowly with as little as thirty seconds of mindfulness meditation at a time. With practice, you will be able to sneak in a little mindfulness more frequently until you are ultimately able to string a whole day's worth of micro meditations together with ease.

Types of micro meditation

- For those with office jobs, one of the easiest ways to practice mindfulness meditation at work is by focusing on the sensations that your fingers provide you as you your hands move across the keyboard. Note the rhythmic sound of the keys being pressed and pay special attention to the feeling of your fingers pressing down on each individual key. Consider carefully how your mind forms each word prior to your fingers making it a reality and spend some extra time thinking about the connection between mind and body that is taking place as well as how it is so often taken for granted.

- If you find yourself sitting for most of the day, prior to starting your micro-meditation it is important to consider your posture. Start by relaxing your entire body starting with your neck and working your way down to your toes before reversing the process and starting at the bottom and working your way up. Once you are relaxed focus on the signals that your body is sending you in an effort to pinpoint any areas that are crying out to you in pain. With the problem points identified you are then going to want to adjust your posture until you are completely pain free.

- If you spend a majority of your day responding to emails or various phone notifications then you can simply add thirty seconds between each reply to center yourself and practice mindfulness in its most minute form. While thirty seconds here or there isn't going to do very much good all on its own, the cumulative effect will surprise you. For example, if you respond to eighty requests requiring your response per day then you are actually spending forty minutes of your day being mindful. Give it a try and you will soon realize just how effective this practice can be if you keep it up.

- If your job requires rote repetition then any time you are performing a mundane task you will find that it is an excellent opportunity to practice being mindful. Any activity that mixes physical activity with an ability to only focus on the specifics of what you are doing in a passive way is essentially a free pass to be mindful. All you need to do is focus entirely on the current task and you will be able to easily fill your day with mindful thoughts.

- If your job requires you to constantly interact with coworkers then you can practice mindfulness by simply devoting all of your mental energy to listening to what the other person has to say. While you might not always appreciate your coworkers' insights, giving them the full scope of your attention will allow you to find a state of mindfulness while at the same time allowing them to feel as though you really care about whatever it is that they are saying.

Additionally, this is a good opportunity to practice improving your overall level of empathy as you can use each conversation as an opportunity to try to determine the other person's mindset in an effort to empathize with their position. Remember, the goal here is to focus on the conversation you are having to such an extent that everything else leaves your mind, you won't be able to multitask but others are sure to see your interpersonal skills go through the roof. During these conversations, you are going to want to give some thought to your body language as well, avoid crossing your arms to ensure you appear open to what the other person has to say. You will also want to consider the amount of space between you and the other party as you don't want to interpose any objects between you nor do you want to end the conversation at a distance that is much greater than where you started.

- In order to maximize the effectiveness of your end of the day commute and the mindfulness meditation you are hopefully practicing therein, you should use the last few minutes of the workday to compartmentalize everything that has happened during the time you were hard at work. Consider what you have managed to accomplish, reflect on your successes and your failures in light of the bigger picture and consider what they mean overall for the days to come. With that done, mentally close the door on the workday and remind yourself that any work problems won't need to be solved until tomorrow. Close the book on the workday before you leave your place of business and you will find your next session of mindfulness meditation to be much more effective than it otherwise might be. Above all, repeat the mantra that tomorrow is another day and another opportunity to get everything right.

While it might seem that making an effort to practice mindfulness in the office will lead to an overall decrease in productivity, the reality is that the opposite is true. Especially if you have a particularly hectic job you likely find that you often have to react to things without thinking through all the possible outcomes of your response. With your head cleared from frequent micro-meditations, however, you will find that the moments in which you have to make important decisions naturally seem to expand in order to provide you with all the time you need to make the right choice, right now.

Remember, when you react to something you at taking a nearly automatic action, letting the stimuli that sent you down this path take control of the situation. However, if you respond instead of react then you are making a well-reasoned choice based on all available data. Reasoned responses lead to better solutions every single time.

With enough time spent practicing mindfulness at work, you will also find that you have gained the ability to approach problems both old and new in ways that you had previously never considered. This will only be the case, however, if you stop thinking about incidents that require your attention as problems and instead consider them in the framework of challenges to be overcome. Problems are simply roadblocks to success while challenges, on the other hand, are incidents that can be learned from and bested for the betterment of you and your place of business. When you come across a challenge that has you stumped, consider writing it down and focusing on it completely to the exclusion of everything else. If you have been practicing mindfulness regularly you will be surprised at how quickly a previously unthought of solution may reveal itself.

CHAPTER 6
Mindfulness At Home

There is perhaps no easier place to practice mindfulness than in your own home as it is there that you have the greatest level of control over yourself and your surroundings. In fact, once you get in the habit of practicing mindfulness on a regular basis there will hardly be anything that you can do that won't lend itself to practicing mindfulness with nothing more than a little extra thought and a little more practice. Who knows, the ways you can practice mindfulness in the home may even surprise you.

Practice mindfulness while taking care of everyday chores

Prior to beginning your journey to understand mindfulness meditation you likely considered taking care of your household chores to be the epitome of drudgery and menial labor. Once you look at them through the lens of mindfulness meditation, however you will soon find that they are one of the best opportunities to practice mindfulness meditation while still being outwardly productive to boot. Remember, any activity that has a physical component that doesn't require your full and active attention can easily become an outlet for mindfulness meditation as long as you approach it in the right way.

When it is time to tackle your chores, the first thing that you are going to want to do is to take a few moments before hand to clear your mind and get in touch with the signals that your body is sending you. With your mind primed, dive into the moment to moment nature of the activity you are pursuing with the goal of limiting thought to the extreme. Instead, consider the way your hands feel as they go through the motions of whatever it is you are doing.

Consider the information your eyes are providing you as the task alters the physical world in one way or another as well as the smells that accompany the task and what it is that they signify. Finally, once you are completed take another moment to enjoy the feeling of accomplish that is sure to manifest from a job well done and consider the difference of the before and after nature of the task you just completed. For the best results, prepare everything you need to do for several chores beforehand so that you can string the periods of mindfulness together as much as possible.

With practice, you can easily create a state of mindfulness that lasts for an hour, if not more.

Practice mindfulness while you are bathing

It doesn't matter if your bathing habits skew towards the morning or the evening, you can easily use this time to practice mindfulness meditation and either help you get ready to start your day off right or to further decompress when the day is at an end. While most people rush through their daily bath or shower with nary a thought, this period of time is rife with sensations for your body to track while at the same time being devoid of any of the distractions that might plague your mindfulness meditation in other settings.

Before you begin your bathing ritual take an extra moment to center yourself and get in touch with your body. If it is early in the morning make an effort to put off all thoughts of the day ahead and if it is evening push out everything that has happened during the day in an effort to get into the moment as quickly as possible. Once you are ready, start by considering the feel of the water on your skin and how the hot, or cold, water feels engulfing your body completely and running down your skin.

Use the repetitive tasks that you are performing as a gateway to reach a mental state that is free of anything but the sensations you are feeling right now. Smell is also an extremely powerful sense in this instance and focusing on the scents that surround you is also a fantastic way to push out other thoughts as they try to intrude.

Practice mindfulness while exercising

While it might seem surprising, the mindset of the average individual who is exercising is already remarkably similar to the mindset of someone who is practicing mindfulness meditation. This is caused by the fact that exercise automatically pushes the sensations that the body is sending out to the forefront of the mind and the concentration that many types of exercise require in order to see the best results. As such, it then only takes a little push to tip this type of mindset over into mindfulness meditation in its entirety. As an added bonus studies show that those who practice mindfulness while they exercise are known to report an increase in their level of endurance as well as a measurable boost to their overall performance.

The key to pushing the one into the other is to reduce your focus on getting everything you are doing exactly right and to instead focus on the body parts that you are pushing to their limits, how they feel as they move and the sensations they are providing you with as you put them through their paces. Each time you complete an exercise and move onto the next you can use the pause in the forward momentum as an opportunity to refocus your attention on the moment and banish any stray thoughts that may have crept in while your focus was elsewhere.

While you are focusing on the moment it is important to not lose track of what you are doing entirely as you may push yourself too hard and accidentally cause undue strain on your body. With that in mind, it doesn't matter what type of exercise you enjoy or where you perform it, there are likely going to be a whole host of sights, sounds and smells to draw you into the moment as thoroughly as possible. For the best results, start off with a focus on what it is you are doing and let yourself get into a rhythm. From there, let your body take care of itself and use the sensations the exercise provides to push everything else out of your mind so that you can find the sense of inner peace that you are striving for.

Practice being mindful while utilizing social media

Despite the fact that it might seem counterintuitive, if you make a concentrated effort to do so, you can even practice mindfulness meditation while you are utilizing social media of all types. While the siren's call of a social media notification can easily draw you out of the moment during several types of mindfulness meditation, if you allocate a set time with which to check up on what your friends are doing you can actually find a state of mindfulness while doing so.

For this type of mindfulness meditation to work, the first thing that you are going to want to do is to eliminate any other potential distractions before you get to work. This is an extremely crucial step due to the fact that a majority of people check social media sites as a means of multitasking. With any distractions out of the way, you will first want to clear your mind and make an effort to inhabit the moment as much as possible. With the proper mindset obtained you can then look at the pictures or text that relates to your personal history with an eye towards inhabiting those past moments as thoroughly as possible.

For every picture that you see or tweet that you read consider what was taking place at its time of inception. Remember the way you felt at the time and let the memory wash over you completely. Make an effort to put yourself into the time and place in question by remembering the various signals that your body was providing you with at the time. Once you have this in mind, you will then want to go even deeper into the memory by starting with the smells you can remember. If the day was hot or cold, try and conjure up the way the temperature felt on your skin and if it was loud, consider what it is your ears were taking in. With enough practice, you will find that you are able to block out all external stimuli and exist solely in a previous moment.

Practice reflecting on the preceding day in a mindful fashion
Prior to going to bed at the end of the day you may find it helpful to practice mindfulness meditation, especially if you have difficulty falling asleep or staying asleep due to stresses that come up naturally during the day. This process of offloading your stress from the day can be done either by taking a mental inventory, but you may find the process more beneficial if you instead write down what has been troubling you.

As usual, you will want to begin by taking a few moments to center yourself and to work to get into the type of mindset that will make it easier to find a state of mindfulness once you get into the bulk of the exercise. When you get ready to write down what you remember about your day you may find it helpful to write out by hand what you remember rather than typing up a journal as the tactile experience of writing can be an easy way to tie yourself to the moment. Likewise, when you want to go back and read what you have previously written you will have that tactile experience of writing it the first time to reflect on in addition to focusing on what happen in the entry that you are reading.

When you start writing it is important that you take stock of the day as a whole and make an effort to include absolutely everything that happened to you in the past twenty-four hours, regardless of how meaningless it seems at the time. As you write you are going to want to commit yourself to remembering each moment as fully as possible, complete with all of the various stimuli that were taking place as the memory was made. With practice, this detailed examination of your day will make it easier for you to pick out various sensations that you might have missed while practicing other forms of mindfulness meditation.

Once you have a little bit more perspective on the events that have unfolded and read back through what you have written you will often find that the individual moments that seem the most innocuous have the greatest impact on the future. Once you have written enough journal entries to begin to notice this type of pattern you will then be primed to notice all of the little moments more throughout your day and let moments of mindfulness slip in as well.

Practice mindfulness meditation to start your day out right

No matter how rushed you feel you are in the morning, you can find a few minutes to practice mindfulness meditation if you make a concentrated effort to do so. The easiest way to do so is by taking a few extra moments to really savor your favorite morning drink be it coffee, tea or even soda or an energy drink. What's more, if you shower in the mornings as well, you can string together a group of mindfulness meditation sessions practically from the moment you wake up until you reach your workplace.

From there, if you do it right you can be mindful throughout your day right up until it is time for bed.

The morning mindfulness meditation session is one of the easiest to get the hang of as the first cup of an energizing beverage of the day is naturally more potent than those that follow it as your body has had all the hours you were asleep to get the caffeine out of your system ensuring that the first jolt is the most powerful that you are going to feel throughout the day. This, in turn, naturally draws you into the present more fully, especially if you take the extra time to really appreciate it. Remember, this may be the only truly relaxing moment of your entire day, it is best to make it count.

For the best results, you are going to want to wake up with the idea of mindfulness on the brain. As you wake in the morning take a few extra moments to consider the thoughts that are already racing through your head and consider why they are there without interacting with them directly. If your thoughts are all about the day ahead, make a concentrated effort to push them aside until you have successfully finished your morning mindfulness meditation routine. If possible, go ahead and slip into a state of mindfulness directly after taking stock of your mental inventory.

Once you are properly adapted to the moment the next thing that you are going to want to do is to pay special attention to the preparation of your drink of choice. While there is certainly going to be more to be aware of if you are grinding coffee beans and filling an espresso machine, even pulling out a teabag or taking a cold drink from the refrigerator has plenty of sensations to offer when it comes to locking you in place in the moment. As you go through the routine of preparation consider the anticipation of what is to come, the smell of the beverage brewing or the feel of the cold can against your skin. Regardless of your drink of choice it is important to really savor the moments before you take your first sip and take in the world around you as much as possible. The goal here is to be able to completely recall the events leading up to your first drink if you are planning to write about it at the end of the day.

Once you are ready to actually take your first drink, you want to find a quiet spot to sit and really appreciate the first sip. Take in the smell of the drink, the smell of it and the feel as it hits your tongue and rolls down your throat. Focus on the feel of the cup or can in your hand and the heat or the cold that is radiating from it. Try and remain in the moment as much as possible and chart the course of the caffeine as it invigorates every part of your body one by one. As you feel the liquid running through your body consider the benefits it is providing you and how it is giving you the energy to face the coming day head on.

During this period, it is important to give the beverage the full sum of your attention, if you find your mind wandering the details of the day simply refocus and bring your mind back to the task at hand. Once you are finished, take note of the way the empty vessel feels now that it is devoid of the precious liquid. Finally, take another few moments to take in the silence around you before readying yourself to start your day in earnest.

Practice dancing or listening to music mindfully
It doesn't matter who you are dancing with or why you are dancing in the first place, dancing itself is an inherently mindful act. Proper dancing requires the complete focus of the dancer both to ensure that the body follows as it should but also of the music, the tempo and the way they work together to affect the

body. If you already love to dance, then all you need to do is be aware of the ways in which it helps you be mindful to take full advantage of their effects.

Much like dancing, playing music in such a way that it demands your attention is an inherently mindful action. As long as you take the time to focus on the moment and consider the way your body relates to the creation of each individual note. Consider the other musicians you are playing with and the ways the smallest change in what you are doing can affect the flow of the whole. For those who are not musically inclined, chanting may be a viable alternative. Repeating a phrase or mantra can be an effective way of achieving a higher state of mindfulness. Like with dancing, an understanding of the mindful principles at play will make you more aware of them in the moment.

Practice being mindful with your family

While oftentimes practicing mindfulness meditation means spending time alone, this isn't a prerequisite for practicing successfully. In fact, practicing mindfulness meditation with your family is actually a great way to spend time with your loved ones, as long as you do it properly that is. The best way to go about doing so is to use group meal times to foster a sense of mindfulness with everyone involved. While it might seem difficult to get multiple people to focus on the moment, as long as things are handled properly, and all technology is left outside the kitchen and/or dining room then the process is easier than you might expect.

First things first, you are going to want to get everyone involved in the preparation for the food, you don't need to make a big deal about the mindfulness aspects inherent in the process, all you need to do is simply encourage everyone to give their full attention to their assigned preparation task. Once everyone has settled into the rhythm of food preparation then you will all be on your way to focusing on the moment to the exclusion of all else.

Once the food is prepared, gather everyone around the table and, before anyone takes their first bite, take a few moments to start your deep breathing exercises and consider all of the sensations that the fresh meal is sending to your body. The first few times you try this with your family you will want to point out the sights of the meal that you have prepared as well as the smells that are wafting out from it. Eventually, this will become simply another part of the meal and you won't have to break your own state of mindfulness to ensure that everyone else is following along.

In addition to taking in the preliminary sights and smells of the meal you will want to make eye contact with each member of your family and as you do so contemplate the special connection that you both share thanks to the meal you have helped prepare together and encourage family members to do the same with everyone else. Finally, you will want to audibly express your gratitude that you can all be together right here, right now, in this particular moment in time.

With the preliminary mindfulness meditation out of the way, it will then be time to get to the main event, the consumption of the meal that you have all come together to prepare for one another. Prior to starting you will want to make a point of cautioning your family to avoid eating to rapidly and to instead make an effort to really taste each bite of food you take, and enjoy the sensations it provides.

As you eat you will want to anchor yourself to the moment by considering all of the flavors that the food provides, feel your teeth tear into it and break it down and feel any spices that may be used as they create a physical sensation in your mouth. You will want to picture each bite as it moves into your stomach and consider the various vitamins and nutrients that it is passing on to your body.

If you try hard enough, you should be able to taste the whole of the universe in every bite. Focus on this thought as you eat and consider the joy you feel when receiving the bounty of the universe and sharing it with the people you love. Breaking bread with someone forms a unique bond with that person quite unlike anything else, consider this as you eat and focus on the moment to ensure it lasts as long as possible.

Another good thing about making a habit out of eating mindfully is that it will naturally draw you to meal options that are naturally healthier overall as processed foods that are full of artificial preservatives don't typically require enough preparation to draw in the entire family. Not only will a careful consideration of the food you eat lead you to feel full more quickly than you otherwise will, such a careful consideration of the food will also often make the meal taste more delicious than those meals which are consumed quickly and without a second thought. As you get more in touch with what you are eating you will also find that it is much easier to determine if you are really in need of sustenance or if you are considering eating for some other, less healthy, alternative.

One downside of practicing mindfulness meditation with the entire family is that if one or more members aren't on board, the exercise loses much of its potency. As such, you are going to want to take special care to ensure that everyone is on the same page for the best results. In order to do this, you may want to start by explaining that the food that you are about to eat is a direct gift from the universe at large. By explaining every step that was required for the food to get from where it was created all the way to your table you will add a weight to the meal that is often lost when people are disproportionately disassociated from their food as most people are in this day and age.

While the preparation of the meal and the first few minutes once you all sit down to eat should be relatively quiet, that doesn't mean that the entire meal should be consumed in silence. If this were the case then you would be little better off than eating alone.

You will, however, want to make it a point to keep conversation focused on the meal itself. To get the ball rolling you are going to want to foster conversation about the quality of the meal, its nutritional value and the general bounty of what has been provided for you. While you won't always be able to keep the conversation in this sphere, you will want to make a point of avoiding any negative conversation or heated debates as these types of topics will only make it more difficult for everyone to remain mindful throughout the meal.

While eating mindfully will likely make each meal seem as though it lasts longer than you are used to, the reality of the situation is that a mindful meal should last no longer, or be any larger, than a normal meal and may actually even be smaller than the meals that you were eating before as your greater level of concentration will often allow you to eat smaller meals while feeling just as full as you otherwise would.

CHAPTER 8
Tips For Improving Your Ability To Be Mindful

Don't focus on your mind

For many people, especially those who are new to mindfulness meditation, the idea of clearing your mind can be exceedingly confusing if not apparently impossible. This is perfectly understandable, especially as it is very difficult for anyone, even mindfulness experts to clear their minds of absolutely all thoughts. Instead of worry that you are doing something wrong, you will find better success if you simply focus on receiving as much information from your senses as possible and let your mind take care of itself. Remember, as long as you are feeling the benefits of mindfulness meditation there is no single right or wrong way to practice it.

Don't worry about finding the "perfect" position

While there are certainly various positions that make the practice of mindfulness meditation easier than others, there is no one perfect position that is suddenly going to pull you into the moment. Rather than looking for an ideal position that is right for all types of mindfulness meditation, you should focus on finding a position that you can hold for a prolonged period of time that doesn't promote any aches or pains that may ultimately distract you from your true goal. Remember, while you want to choose a position that is relaxing, you also don't want to find one that is so relaxing that it causes you to fall asleep. Work on finding a position that straddles the line somewhere in the middle in order to see the best results.

Ensure you are focusing properly

If you are having a difficult time bringing your consciousness to the moment, the first thing you are going to want to do is to put all of your focus into feeling your breath. If you find that the feeling of air moving in through your nose and out through your mouth isn't enough to keep your mind focused, you may have better luck focusing on what your abdominal muscles instead. As such, instead of focusing on the breath itself, focus on the sensation of breathing in and out that is provided by the muscles in your abdomen expanding and contracting.

Don't get ahead of yourself

With so many different ways to practice being mindful, it can be easy for those who are new to the practice to want to jump straight into one of the more complicated types of meditation straight out of the gate. Then, when they have trouble achieving a state of mindfulness they get discouraged and give up before they have experienced any of the benefits that meditation can provide. As such, it is best to start off slowly with the basic form of mindfulness meditation and practice existing in the moment when there are no distractions around before moving to a more advanced version of the exercise.

Don't get discouraged when your mind wanders

For many new mindfulness meditation practitioners controlling a wandering mind can seem like an impossible task. This is a perfectly normal feeling and it is important that you work through this early stage with perseverance and hard work if you ever hope to reap the benefits that mindfulness meditation provides. There is no trick to this practice, all it takes is lots of repetition and a commitment to always bringing your mind back into focus as soon as it begins to wander.

Be prepared for intense emotions

While not everyone is going to experience extreme emotions while practicing mindfulness meditation, it is important to be aware of the potential for doing so in order to be prepared if it does happen to you. Intense feelings of joy are common but, on the other hand, some practitioners have also experienced sudden bouts of anger, fear, grief or depression. The important thing to remember is that these feelings aren't indicative of your overall mental state and that only by focusing on the moment as fully as possible can you prevent them from interrupting your feeling of mindfulness.

Don't focus on the results, focus on the experience
Mindfulness meditation can provide a wide variety of benefits for those that practice it on a regular basis. However, that doesn't mean that you are going to start experiencing everything that mindfulness meditation has to offer as soon as you start. What's worse, practicing with one eye planted firmly in the future will make it much more difficult to exist fully in the moment and, as a result, push any results you might see even further into the future. Focus on getting to a point where you can exist in the moment and let everything else take care of itself.

Don't let negative thoughts fester

One of the greatest impediments to successful mindfulness meditation are negative or stressful thoughts that tend to cloud the mind and make it difficult to listen to the signals that your body is sending you. As such, for the best results, you are going to want to make a concentrated effort to let go of these types of thoughts before you start meditating otherwise they are likely to draw your focus away from what you should be doing.

Understand the physical changes that your mind is going through

While you are training your brain to be more mindful it is important to understand just what it is you are actually doing and to do that you need to understand the basics of how the brain works. Specifically, habits are formed because neurons move through the brain via the path of least resistance. The more that a given neural pathway is used (by repetition of a given thought or action) the more likely the neurons in the brain are going to use that path in the future. When you make a concentrated effort to be more mindful on a daily basis you are creating new neural pathways and the only way to ensure that they are used regularly is to practice, practice, practice.

Don't worry about a little numbness

In most situations, if you find that your leg or legs have gone to sleep, the most common response is to reposition yourself to ensure that blood starts flowing to the affected area in a greater quantity. While no one is suggesting that you cut off the blood flow to your limbs completely, if you are only practicing mindfulness meditation for fifteen or thirty minutes at a time then a bit of numbness can be a powerful tool when it comes to helping you focus on the moment. Remember, mindfulness meditation is all about using sensations, all sensations, to anchor yourself in the moment as fully as possible. Don't be too anxious to shut out sensations that you are feeling, even if they are typically considered to be negative.

Handle distractions properly

While you likely won't encounter many distractions when you are practicing mindfulness meditation at home, the greater the variety of places that you practice meditating in, the more likely you are to be interrupted when you are in the middle of connecting to the moment. When this occurs, it is important to treat the distraction as you would any other errant thought and simply let it float away until you can continue whatever it was you were doing. While often easier said than done, it is important to approach distractions in this fashion as otherwise you are likely to let your emotions get the best of you and once that happens it will be even more difficult to get back into the state that you were in before the distraction first brought itself to your attention.

Take care to avoid drowsiness

It is perfectly natural for the process of mindfulness meditation to lead to a feeling of drowsiness, especially if you are practicing at the end of a long day. If you hope to get the most out of the practice you are going to want to avoid this feeling as much as possible which may mean taking extra precautions before you get started. Specifically, you are going to want to avoid eating heavy meals before you begin your mindfulness meditation practice or exercising to the point of exhaustion. If you still find yourself becoming drowsy, turn the focus of your mind from the body to the mind itself and try and probe the edges of your mind in an effort to determine just what sensations being drowsy provides. If, after fifteen minutes or so, if the feeling persists you may want to find something else to do for a time until the feeling passes.

Don't seek comparison with others

While the basic practice of mindfulness meditation is relatively universal, the end results from practicing on a regular basis are going to be dramatically different for everyone who gives mindfulness a serious try. As such, rather than wasting your time comparing your results to the results of others, you will have a more productive experience if you focus all of that curious energy and double down on your own mindfulness meditation practice. If you are trying to analyze what you are trying to do, or what you are potentially doing wrong, then you are not going to be truly in the moment and the results you are looking for will be forever out of reach. Rather, you will note better results in the long run if you choose to simply meditate as effectively as you can and trust that the practice will lead to the types of results that you are looking for.

CONCLUSION

Thank for making it through to the end of *Mindfulness Meditation for Self-Healing: Beginner's Meditation Guide to Eliminate Stress and Anxiety, and Find Inner Peace and Happiness,* let's hope it was informative and able to provide you with all of the tools you need to achieve your goals relating to mindfulness meditation whether it is something that you are interested in doing just once in a while or if you are hoping to reach a point where a majority of each and every day is spent being as fully committed to being focused on the present as humanly possible. Just because you've finished this book doesn't mean there is nothing left to learn on the topic, expanding your horizons is the only way to find the mastery you seek.

The next step is to stop reading and to get started practicing mindfulness meditation as frequently as possible. While initially you may not feel as though you are getting very much out of the time that you put in, the more you keep at it the more quickly the positive benefits of being mindful are going to start stacking up. Don't get discouraged if at first you find that your mind remains unruly, every moment you spend fully engrossed in the moment will make it easier to reach the desired mental state in the future. Take it one step at a time and you will soon find yourself fully engaged in the present without even trying.

There are so many different types of mindfulness meditation that, as long as you keep at it, you are bound to find something that works for you sooner or later. The only way that you won't be able to get anything out of mindfulness meditation is if you give up before you have tried them all. Remember, it takes at least thirty days for a new routine to become habit, and practice makes perfect!

Finally, if you found this book useful in anyway, a review on Amazon is always appreciated!

www.ingramcontent.com/pod-product-compliance
Lightning Source LLC
Chambersburg PA
CBHW071509070526
44578CB00001B/490